VIRGINIA WOOLF

VIRGINIA WOOLF

Sue Asbee

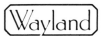

Life and Works

Jane Austen
The Brontës
Thomas Hardy
Hemingway
D.H. Lawrence
Katherine Mansfield
George Orwell
Shakespeare
H.G. Wells
Virginia Woolf

Cover illustration by David Armitage

First published in 1989 by
Wayland (Publishers) Ltd
61 Western Road, Hove,
East Sussex BN3 1JD, England

Series adviser: Dr Cornelia Cook
Series designer: David Armitage
Editor: Sophie Davies

British Library Cataloguing in Publication Data
Asbee, Sue
   Virginia Woolf.- (Life & Works)
   1. Fiction in English, Woolf, Virginia,
   1882-1941
   I. Title II. Series
   823'.912 [F]

   ISBN 1 85210 676 X

Typeset by: Kalligraphics Ltd, Horley, Surrey
Printed in Italy by: G. Canale C.S.p.A., Turin
Bound in the UK by Maclehose & Partners, Portsmouth

Contents

1 The Writer's Life

Family life

Virginia Woolf wrote novels, short stories, essays, biography and literary criticism. Her letters and diaries have been edited and published. Her fiction is important enough to make her private life interesting, and understanding her background helps to show us why she addressed particular subjects in particular ways.

Woolf's family life helps to explain how her views on male dominance were formed, together with the desire to change things, which is a major theme in her essays and fiction. After a happy early childhood, a series of deaths in her family brought periods of depression and mental breakdown, with which she was to struggle throughout her life. Undoubtedly she drew on these experiences when writing her fiction.

She was born Adeline Virginia Stephen, in London on 25 January 1882. Her family was a large one; her parents, Leslie and Julia Stephen, had both been married and widowed before. Julia's first husband Herbert Duckworth had died, leaving her three children, George, Stella and Gerald to care for. Virginia described them as ' "the others" . . . not brothers and sister, but beings possessed of knives, or enviable gifts for running or carving'; to her they were both 'tyrants and demi-gods'.

Leslie Stephen, a famous Victorian man of letters, had been married to Harriet Thackeray, the novelist's daughter, until her death in 1875. Leslie lived in the same street as Julia, and when they married in 1878 she and

Opposite *Virginia Stephen at the age of twenty-one.*

Stella Duckworth holding her baby step-sister, Vanessa.

the Duckworth children moved into 22 Hyde Park Gate with Leslie, and Laura, his mentally handicapped daughter. Within five years, Vanessa, Thoby, Virginia and Adrian were born.

Nurses and children in Kensington Gardens. Virginia recalled that she and her brothers and sisters spent much of their time here.

Stella, Gerald and George Duckworth, Virginia's step-sister and brothers, whom she later described as 'tyrants and demi-gods'.

'Our life,' Virginia wrote:

. . . was ordered with great simplicity and regularity. It seemed to divide itself into two large spaces . . . One space was spent indoors, in the drawing room and nursery, and the other in Kensington Gardens.

(*Moments of Being*, p.32-3)

Their brothers went to school, but like Stella, Vanessa and Virginia had little formal education beyond drawing, dancing and music: accomplishments that the daughters of gentlemen were expected to acquire. There were governesses, but the children were mainly taught by their mother, and later their father, at home. The brothers were expected to go to university, the girls to marry. Virginia's own experience may not have been quite so unsympathetic, but a discussion of a brother and sister in her first novel *The Voyage Out* (1915), shows her awareness of the discrepancy between boys' and girls' education:

> . . . not a day's passed since we came here without a discussion as to whether he's going to stay on at Cambridge or to go to the Bar. It's his career – his sacred career . . . Can't you imagine the family conclaves, and the sister told to run out and feed the rabbits because St John must have the schoolroom to himself – 'St John's working', 'St John wants his tea brought to him'. No wonder that St John thinks it a matter of some importance. It is too. He has to earn a living. But St John's sister . . . No one takes her seriously, poor dear. She feeds the rabbits.
>
> (*The Voyage Out*, p.213)

Longing to have a foothold in the world that Thoby inhabited, Virginia began lessons in Greek. Her father allowed her to read anything from his library, but as she 'gobbled' Dickens, George Eliot, Carlyle and Pepys, Macauley's *History* and Thomas Arnold's *History of Rome*, he stressed: 'My dear, if it's worth reading, it's worth reading twice.' He insisted that she formed her own opinions, and that she learned to express herself economically: valuable lessons which she remembered all her life.

From the age of nine, with Thoby, Virginia produced *The Hyde Park Gate News*, a journal of their day-to-day life, for the family to read. Vanessa's passion was for drawing, Virginia's always for writing.

The house at Hyde Park Gate was a large six-storey home, run in conventional upper-middle-class style, with nurses for the children as well as at least seven maidservants. Each summer from 1882 until Virginia

Opposite *Virginia Stephen with her younger brother Adrian. Virginia was to write with some bitterness about the difference between boys' and girls' education.*

was twelve years old, the entire family went to St Ives in Cornwall for the summer.

> Probably nothing we had as children was quite so important to us as our summers in Cornwall . . . to hear the waves breaking that first night behind the yellow blind; to sail in the lugger; to dig in the sands; to scramble over the rocks and see the anemones flourishing their antennae in the pools . . .
>
> (*Moments of Being*, p.128)

The childhood holidays acted upon her imagination, forming the background to *To the Lighthouse* (1927), as well as being recognizable in *Jacob's Room* (1922) and *The Waves* (1931).

When Virginia was thirteen, her mother died. The whole household was plunged into deep mourning, and the cherished holidays came to an end. Julia was 49 years old, and worn out by the constant demands of her husband and children, as well as countless social interests – such as work among the poor and unemployed. Many years later Virginia wrote: '. . . she died easily of overwork at 49: he [her father] found it difficult to die of cancer at 72.'

Leslie reproached himself with failing to demonstrate the depth of his love for his wife, and it was his step-daughter Stella who bore the main burden of listening to his confessions and misery, as well as assuming her mother's role of presiding over the household. Her engagement to Jack Hills the following year helped to lighten the 'melodramatic, histrionic and unreal' funereal gloom which hung over the family. However, three months after her marriage in 1897, pregnant, Stella died from appendicitis.

It was from her observations of her father's demands, first on his wife, then on his step-daughter, and ultimately on Vanessa, the next female in line, that Virginia formed early notions of male dominance and female oppression. She loved her father dearly, but wrote that, at the time, she and Vanessa:

> . . . made him into the type of all that we hated in our lives; he was the tyrant of inconceivable selfishness, who had replaced the beauty and merriment of the dead

Opposite *Julia Stephen, Virginia's mother. She died 'of overwork' at the age of 49, when her daughter was thirteen.*

12

with ugliness and gloom . . . there was some truth in
our complaint.

(*Moments of Being*, p.65)

If the holidays in St Ives formed the background of *To the Lighthouse*, the relationship between Virginia's parents provided the model for Mr and Mrs Ramsay, the central characters in that novel. After Mrs Ramsay's death, her husband longs for sympathy:

> . . . this was one of those moments when an enormous need urged him, without being conscious of what it was, to approach any woman, to force them, he did not care how, his need was so great, to give him what he wanted: sympathy.

(To the Lighthouse, p.142)

Lily, a painter and guest of the Ramsay family, is oppressed by his presence:

> . . . she could do nothing. Every time he approached – he was walking up and down the terrace – ruin approached, chaos approached. She could not paint. She took up this rag; she squeezed that tube . . . He made it impossible for her to do anything.

Opposite Stella Duckworth, who bore the brunt of Leslie Stephen's despair and need for sympathy after her mother's death. She herself died from appendicitis during pregnancy two years later.

Leslie Stephen, Virginia's father, a well-known man of letters. He inspired the character Mr Ramsay in To the Lighthouse.

Virginia with her favourite brother Thoby, in 1900. Thoby's death from typhoid fever in 1906 was one of the shocks that triggered Virginia's mental illness, and led to the obsession with sudden death in her writing.

Death and madness

The first of the mental breakdowns, from which Virginia was to suffer intermittently all her life, occurred after her mother's death. She had severe headaches, was nervous, excitable and deeply distressed by turns; and worse, she heard 'horrible voices'. Treatment always meant complete rest from all work, both reading and writing. Partly for this reason, Virginia's diaries tell us nothing of her illness. However, she certainly drew on her experiences in her fiction. Her mother and step-sister died before she was fifteen, her father when she was twenty-two. Thoby died of typhoid fever two years after that. Her acquaintance with death was as an observer, mental breakdown she knew from within.

Virginia was deeply affected by these deaths, and there are many sudden deaths in her fiction. Rachel, at the end of *The Voyage Out*, dies after illness and delirium; Jacob Flanders dies at the end of *Jacob's Room*. Percival – like Jacob, a portrait of her brother Thoby – dies a pointless and sudden death in *The Waves*. Like Rhoda's suicide in the same novel, this death is reported: we are given the bare facts of the accident, and there is no attempt to describe how he or Rhoda might have felt. Similarly, Mrs Ramsay's death in *To the Lighthouse* is described only in terms of her husband's need for her.

Her death is a shock to the reader, and we are not told how or why she died:

> . . . Mr Ramsay stumbling along a passage stretched his arms out one dark morning, but Mrs Ramsay having died rather suddenly the night before, he stretched his arms out. They remained empty.

(To the Lighthouse, p.120)

Death in Woolf's fiction is arbitrary and inexplicable. It is in the character of Septimus Smith, in *Mrs Dalloway*, however, that she comes closest to describing her own experiences. Septimus suffers guilt and madness because 'he could not feel'. Witnessing the death of his officer Evans in the First World War (1914–18) Septimus: 'far from showing any emotion or recognizing that here was the end of a friendship, congratulated himself upon feeling very little and very reasonably' (*Mrs Dalloway*, p.78). This repression is largely responsible for his mental illness. In later life Virginia described a similarly inappropriate response when, taken to her mother's deathbed, she had a distinct desire to laugh. Like Septimus, in the period of mental breakdown following this, she heard the birds singing in Greek:

> He listened. A sparrow perched on the railing opposite chirped Septimus, Septimus, four or five times over and went on, drawing its notes out, to sing freshly and piercingly in Greek words how there is no crime and, joined by another sparrow, they sang in voices prolonged and piercing in Greek words . . . how there is no death.

(Mrs Dalloway, p.23-4)

A lone soldier amid the destruction of the First World War, on the Amiens-St Quentin Road, 1917. In Mrs Dalloway, *Septimus' repression of his experiences during the war leads to his mental illness.*

Like Virginia, Septimus is mistrustful of doctors. Indeed, it is to escape Dr Holmes, a man capable of 'forcing your soul', that he flings himself out of a window to his death. His feelings remain confused even as he does so: 'He did not want to die. Life was good' (*Mrs Dalloway* p.132).

After her father's death in 1904 Virginia made a suicide attempt, but fortunately the window from which she jumped was not high enough for her to sustain serious injury. Another attempt, by overdose, after her marriage, and as she finished her first novel, nearly proved fatal. It was not until 1941 when she was 61 years old that, hearing those terrible voices in her head again, and aware that she was about to sink into another period of madness, Virginia weighted her pockets with stones and drowned herself in the River Ouse, close to her home.

Virginia with Clive Bell, Vanessa's husband, in 1910. Virginia was recovering from a bout of serious mental illness.

Bloomsbury

Leslie Stephen's death issued in a new era. While Virginia was away from home recovering from a breakdown, Vanessa sold the house and moved into 46 Gordon Square in Bloomsbury, London. When Virginia arrived, the claustrophobic Victorian atmosphere – the black paint, red plush and heavy William Morris wallpaper – was a thing of the past; the new house was white, light and airy. 'Everything was going to be new; everything was going to be different. Everything was on trial' (*Moments of Being*, p.188). Thoby brought friends home from Cambridge University, and thus what has since become known as 'The Bloomsbury Group' came into being. Lytton Strachey, E.M. Forster, Saxon Sydney-Turner, Clive Bell, Duncan Grant and Leonard Woolf gathered at Gordon Square to discuss philosophy, art and religion.

The writer Henry James described Lytton and Saxon as 'Deplorable! Deplorable!' and asked how Leslie's daughters could have picked up such friends. But for Virginia the young men's shabbiness was both reassuring and a symbol of their superiority:

> They criticized our arguments as severely as their own. They never seemed to notice how we were dressed or if we were nice looking or not. All that tremendous encumbrance of appearance and behaviour which George [their step-brother] had piled upon our first years vanished completely. One had no longer to endure that terrible inquisition after a party – and to be told 'You looked lovely'. Or, 'You did look plain'. Or 'You really must learn to do your hair' . . . all this seemed to have no meaning or existence in the world of Bell, Strachey, Hawtrey and Sydney-Turner.

(*Moments of Being*, p.195)

Saxon Sydney-Turner, Clive Bell and Virginia Stephen in Dorset, 1910. The group of friends who met and talked at Virginia and Vanessa's house in Gordon Square later became known as the 'Bloomsbury Group'.

The intellectual atmosphere and freedom from the conventions of polite society were a breath of fresh air, but in spite of Virginia's 'reassurance', romance inevitably entered the arena. Vanessa married Clive Bell and later had an affair with Duncan Grant, who was the father of her third child. Lytton Strachey, a homosexual, proposed to Virginia, only to withdraw his offer of marriage the next day. They remained life-long friends. Leonard Woolf was a writer and a novelist; when he proposed to Virginia, in 1912, she accepted, and they settled into a companionable, though not passionate, life together. Early in their marriage Leonard was faced with the decision of whether or not to have Virginia certified as insane. Instead, he decided not to, and devoted himself to her care, providing her with peace and quiet when she most needed it. Together they started the Hogarth Press, publishing short stories of their own. Eventually the press published all of Virginia's novels, and also such important works of the modernist movement as T.S. Eliot's *The Waste Land*.

Clive Bell, Desmond MacCarthy, Marjorie Strachey and Virginia. Marjorie is holding a 'Votes for Women' pamphlet.

Opposite *Lytton Strachey, a leading member of the Bloomsbury Group, proposed to Virginia in 1909, but later withdrew his proposal.*

'A Sketch of the Past'

Two years before her death, Virginia wrote 'A Sketch of the Past', an account of her early life. Although it is autobiographical, it raises many of the themes and concerns of her fiction. She begins by saying how difficult the task is: she remembers such a lot, and could write her memoirs in so many different ways, but she plunges in and begins with 'the first memory'. This is not of a specific incident, but of:

> . . . red and purple flowers on a black ground – my mother's dress; and she was sitting either in a train or in an omnibus, and I was on her lap. Perhaps we were going to St Ives; more probably, for from the light it must have been evening, we were coming back to London. But it is more convenient artistically to suppose we were going to St Ives, for that will lead to my other memory, which also seems to be my first memory . . .

> (*Moments of Being*, p.74)

There are several important ideas here. The first is that artistic truth is more important than establishing facts. One thing must lead into another, the result must be aesthetically pleasing, and mere fact is secondary. Secondly, Woolf is discussing her method of writing within the piece of work that we read. She draws attention to the difficulties of presentation, and incorporates them into her work. This is typical of many of her novels too: Lily Briscoe in *To the Lighthouse* is absorbed with the

St Ives in Cornwall. Virginia's memories of family holidays there influenced much of her writing.

structure of her painting, which in some ways echoes the structure of that novel; Miss La Trobe in *Between the Acts* is a playwright, concerned as Woolf was, to make her audience *see;* Bernard, a storyteller and writer in *The Waves* distrusts 'neat designs of life that are drawn on half sheets of notepaper'. So does Woolf, and she therefore begins her memoirs not with dates and places, but with a memory of flowers on her mother's dress.

This incident is most likely to have occurred while returning to London, but it is appropriate to suppose that, instead, she was setting out to St Ives, for this leads to another important memory, her first night there. In a similar way, Woolf's novels gain their coherence not from incident, plot or story, so much as from memories and the association of ideas.

The 'Sketch' continues:

> If life has a base that it stands upon, if it is a bowl that one fills and fills and fills – then my bowl without a doubt stands upon this memory. It is of lying half asleep, half awake, in bed in the nursery at St Ives. It is of hearing the waves breaking, one, two, one, two, and sending a splash of water over the beach . . .

In the bowl which is filled and filled, not only does Woolf suggest that the past can be as immediate as the present, she also suggests that it is our memories which make us what we are, which give us our identities. This may seem obvious: if you lose your memory, you may not remember your name, family, or where you live. But in Woolf's fiction this insight – that new memories may displace old ones, but anything important will remain, not necessarily in any chronological order – is used to provide the continuity and organization of her material. It is also through memories that a kind of immortality is achieved. Mrs Dalloway for example, is certain that she is part:

> . . . of the trees at home, of the house there, ugly, rambling all to bits and pieces as it was; part of people she had never met; being laid out like a mist between people she knew best, who lifted her on their branches as she had seen the trees lift the mist, but it spread ever so far, her life, herself.

> *(Mrs Dalloway, p.10)*

These insights come, practically enough, as Mrs Dalloway looks into a shop window in a busy London street. She echoes Woolf's own belief:

> . . . that behind the cotton wool is hidden a pattern; that we – I mean all human beings – are connected with this; that the whole world is a work of art; that we are parts of the work of art.

> *(Moments of Being, p.84)*

Brought up without religious beliefs, she turned art into a religion.

Woolf was always aware of the inadequacy of words, the inevitable limitations of language when trying to describe a feeling or sensation. After her description of lying in the nursery, she says that she could spend 'hours' trying to write that memory 'as it should be written'. 'I should fail' she says, for there are always other ways of putting things, which might have been more successful. This sense of 'failure' meant that after completing a novel, she almost always sank into deep depression, however optimistic she may have felt when working on it, and however much critical encouragement Leonard gave her. But it may have been this same feeling of dissatisfaction which drove her to experiment with new forms for each novel.

Opposite *Virginia married Leonard Woolf in August 1912. A writer and critic himself, he greatly encouraged Virginia's writing.*

24

2
Modernism

All human relations have shifted – those between masters and servants, husbands and wives, parents and children. And when human relations change there is at the same time a change in religion, conduct, politics and literature. Let us agree to place one of these changes about the year 1910.

(Virginia Woolf, from the essay 'Mr Bennett and Mrs Brown')

Woolf is known as a 'modernist' writer. Her sense of the world as chaotic and fragmentary, coupled with a desire to find some pattern beneath the surface, and to express both these ideas through her art, is something she shared with contemporaries such as T.S. Eliot, E.M. Forster (both friends of the Woolfs') and with James Joyce. Her refusal to give one single view of anything, offering instead multiple, often conflicting views which the reader has to balance and bring together is a modernist trait. A quotation from *To the Lighthouse* helps to illustrate this:

. . . the waves shape themselves symmetrically from the cliff top, but to the swimmer among them [they] are divided by deep gulfs, foaming crests.

Opposite *Virginia Stephen in 1910. She later wrote that all human relations shifted in that year.*

Neither one view nor the other is 'right'; one's perceptions are always relative.

Innovations in music and the visual arts in the early twentieth century show that modernism was not confined to writing. Nevertheless, it was not a 'movement' with accepted ideas laid down by a group of like-minded writers, artists or composers. Rather it was the result of dissatisfaction with the way things had been presented in the past. Victorian novelists had an almost god-like attitude to their characters, using narrators who seemed to know everything there was to know about them, and did not doubt that all this information could be passed on to their readers. For the modernists there was no such certainty.

Thomas Stearns Eliot: poet, playwright and literary critic. His 'The Waste Land' was a major landmark of modernist writing. It was first published by Leonard and Virginia Woolf's company, The Hogarth Press.

E.M. Forster, novelist and literary critic. His writing, like Woolf's, showed a desire to find a pattern beneath the surface of a chaotic and fragmentary reality.

Loss of religious faith meant that, for example, the destruction and turmoil of the First World War could not simply be referred to a God who works his purpose out in mysterious ways beyond out understanding. And if there is no God, how can we be sure that life has any purpose or meaning? 'What did it mean?' is a question repeated again and again by narrator and characters alike in Woolf's fiction.

Modernist attitudes
were greatly
influenced by the
turmoil and
destruction of the
First World War.

The psychoanalysts Freud and Jung were publishing
their work, as was William James (brother of Henry
James, the novelist), so there was a new interest in
psychology and the ways in which our minds work.
This fired the imagination of writers who were searching
for new ways of representing thought, in writing that
was fluid and associative, rather than straightforward
and logical. 'Life', Woolf wrote in 'Modern Fiction':

Opposite *Sigmund*
Freud (1856–1939),
the founder of
psychoanalysis.

. . . is not a series of gig-lamps symmetrically arranged;
life is a luminous halo, a semi-transparent envelope sur-
rounding us from the beginning of consciousness to
the end.

Carl Gustav Jung (1875–1961), psychologist and psychiatrist. The works of Freud and Jung inspired many modernist writers, who were searching for new ways of representing the workings of the mind.

If we read an eighteenth-century novel, Woolf says, using Daniel Defoe's *Robinson Crusoe* as an example: '. . . we are trudging a plain high road; one thing happens after another and the order of the fact is enough'. In the twentieth century, that is no longer enough:

> The mind receives myriad impressions – trivial, fantastic, evanescent, or engraved with the sharpness of steel. From all sides they come, an incessant shower of innumerable atoms.

In Woolf's opinion it was the work of a modern writer to attempt to capture this type of perception, and that was what she aimed for in her novels.

3
The Novels

The Voyage Out

Woolf's first two novels are conventional in form and structure. In *The Voyage Out* Rachel Vinrace timidly steps out to meet the world of experience; her movement from ignorance to maturity is echoed in the title – a journey which takes her from London to South America, and also, ultimately, to her death – a different kind of voyage. The 'journey-through-life' device is as old as literature itself. It does little to help express the very original subject matter Woolf was dealing with: the difficulty of communication, fear of violation, deep anxiety about sex, marriage as a loss of individuality, and the difference between inner and outer realities.

In The Voyage Out, *Rachel's journey to South America, on a cruise liner like this one, is also a voyage out into the world of experience.*

Rachel is twenty-four years old. Her mother died when she was a child, and she has been brought up by two elderly maiden aunts; the voyage to South America is intended to broaden her outlook. Her conventional education has done nothing to help this process:

> . . . for she had been educated as the majority of well-to-do girls in the last part of the nineteenth century were educated. Kindly doctors and gentle old professors had taught her the rudiments of about ten different branches of knowledge, but they would as soon have forced her to go through one piece of drudgery thoroughly as they would have told her that her hands were dirty.

(*The Voyage Out*, p.29)

Girls receiving a dancing lesson in 1897. Woolf was deeply critical of the fact that girls were taught 'accomplishments' such as dancing, drawing and sewing, while boys had a proper formal education.

The inadequacies of girls' education is a theme that recurs throughout Woolf's writing, from this first novel through to *Three Guineas* (1938), a non-fictional examination of the question 'how can we prevent war?' In *The Voyage Out*, Rachel is entrusted to Helen Ambrose, an older, married woman who thinks when she first meets Rachel that the young woman 'really might be six' – such is the effect of her sheltered life. Under Helen's care, Rachel slowly becomes less shy and serious. She

has had hardly any contact with men – even her father has been absent, as he is captain of a ship. Helen, however, has advanced ideas: 'Talk was the medicine she trusted to, talk about everything, talk that was free, unguarded and candid'. Importantly, she does not encourage in Rachel 'those habits of unselfishness and amiability founded upon insincerity which are put at so high a value in mixed households of men and women'.

Rachel's first real encounter with the opposite sex comes on her voyage to South America. The ship picks up two passengers for part of the journey, Mr and Mrs Dalloway. Woolf wrote about these characters again in *Mrs Dalloway*, though that book is in no way a sequel to *The Voyage Out*. Conversation at dinner is one of the first instances of 'talk that was free' in which Helen places so much faith. Mrs Dalloway, for example, says that she suffers from two contradictory impulses: 'the delights of shutting oneself up in a little world of one's own' and also the need to do something in the world, about poverty, for example. Eventually Rachel retreats into complete isolation, a world of her own that is terrifying and leads to her death. But Richard Dalloway also has an impact on her, for he generates a sense of excitement, and of the unknown, which is then replaced with fear.

The passengers of a ship playing bucket quoits. It is on board ship that Rachel in The Voyage Out *has her first real encounter with the opposite sex.*

A woman traveller in South America. Rachel in The Voyage Out *becomes seriously ill after a jungle expedition. Her delirious state allows Woolf to explore reality as it is perceived by a disturbed mind.*

When they are alone together on deck he kisses her passionately. Rachel's head goes cold, her knees shake, and 'the physical pain of the emotion was so great that she could only keep herself moving above the great leaps of her heart'. Leaning on the rail of the ship and gazing out to sea she becomes more peaceful but at the same time 'possessed with a strange exultation. Life seemed to hold infinite possibilities she had never guessed at'. She gradually becomes calm again, but is aware that 'something wonderful had happened'. This feeling does not endure. At dinner Richard avoids her eyes, and Rachel feels deeply uncomfortable. That night she has a terrible nightmare; as she wakes up, 'light showed her familiar things: her clothes, fallen off the chair; the water jug gleaming white'. But the horror does not go away:

A voice moaned for her; eyes desired her. All night long barbarian men harassed the ship; they came scuffling down the passages, and stopped to snuffle at her door. She could not sleep again.

(*The Voyage Out*, p.74)

There are, of course, no barbarian men on the ship, nor do voices actually moan, or eyes desire her, but Woolf presents these delusions as if they really happened, so closely does the narrative follow Rachel's point of view. Rachel's awareness of sex has been awakened by Dalloway and her innocence can never be recaptured. Her fear of a future which includes men in this new light is shown in her nightmare and her sense of being pursued.

Rachel becomes engaged to a young man called Terence Hewet while she is in South America. The exotic tropical setting does much of the work of expressing the new sensation of falling in love, for Woolf never wrote on such topics with much conviction. It is possible that Rachel picks up her illness on the jungle expedition where they declare their love; one of the other characters suggests this might be the case. But the narrator deliberately fails to make it clear, for though Rachel is looking forward to going back to England and marrying, part of her is unable to accept the idea of union with any man, so her retreat into the private world of delirium can also be seen as an escape. Rachel and Terence become engaged in the jungle; the alien scenery also suggests the realms of the unconscious, so the setting is artistically appropriate, providing both physical and mental reasons for Rachel's illness.

The exotic jungle scenery in The Voyage Out *suggests Rachel's new sexual awareness, as well as the realms of the unconscious that the book explores.*

Her sickness starts with a headache. She gets out of bed, but 'the instability of the floor proved that it would be . . . intolerable to stand'. The narrative technique here is similar to that used to describe Rachel's fear on the ship. It might be more accurate to say: 'the floor *seemed* unstable', but we are focusing on Rachel's point of view, so we experience things as she would: to her it seems as though the floor beneath her feet is unreliable. Later when Terence kisses her, her eyes are open, but '. . . she only saw an old woman slicing a man's head off with a knife'.

After about a week of illness, there is a day when Rachel is conscious of what is happening around her.

> She had come to the surface of the dark sticky pool, and a wave seemed to bear her up and down with it; she had ceased to have a will of her own; she lay on the top of the wave conscious of some pain, but chiefly of weakness. The wave was replaced by the side of a mountain. Her body became a drift of melting snow, above which her knees rose in huge peaked mountains of bare bone.

(*The Voyage Out*, p.353)

She feels as though her body and her mind are quite separate, her body on the bed, while her mind escapes, 'flitting round the room'. She is aware of and recognizes Helen's presence, but it is Terence's which is most disturbing:

> All sights were something of an effort, but the sight of Terence was the greatest effort, because he forced her to join mind to body in the desire to remember something. She did not wish to remember; it troubled her when people tried to disturb her loneliness; she wished to be alone. She wished for nothing else in the world.

(*The Voyage Out*, p.354)

Opposite *Rachel's fear of marriage as a loss of individuality may, it is suggested, be a cause of her mental and physical illness.*

What she does not wish to remember is that she is to be joined to Terence in marriage, because however much she loves him, she knows it would mean the loss of her individuality.

Rachel's separateness from him gave Terence cause for anxiety before her illness. He is jealous of her ability 'to cut herself adrift from him, and to pass away to

unknown places where she had no need of him'. He is with her when she dies, and his first thought is that if this is death, then death is simply ceasing to breathe. 'It was perfect happiness', he thinks, 'they had now what they had always wanted to have, the union which had been impossible while they lived'.

Woolf's presentation of Rachel's delirious state of mind is successful largely because those passages are written as if they are real. To someone in Rachel's state they would be real, as Woolf knew from her own experience. But Woolf is equally successful in showing the extraordinary changes of mood in those caring for the sick. Terence is devoted, solicitous, angry and also irritable while Rachel is ill. He has a moment of ecstatic happiness immediately after her death, but it does not last. When someone enters the room, he speaks first in a tone of complete ordinariness: 'there's a halo round the moon. We shall have rain tomorrow'; but this cannot be sustained either, and it is followed by an outburst of grief.

Night and Day

Woolf's second novel, *Night and Day*, is as conventional in form as *The Voyage Out*. Two pairs of lovers change partners, suffer from misunderstandings, but are destined eventually to marry the 'right' people. Katherine Hilbery is the main character, but in many ways Mary Datchet, the feminist, is as interesting. At the end of the novel she is alone, and her situation and commitment to the cause of suffrage – votes for women – is not romanticized: hers is seen as a relatively hard and lonely life.

The difficulty of ever knowing another human being was something which preoccupied Woolf throughout her writing career. In *Night and Day* this difficulty is expressed with particular reference to Katherine. Ralph Denham falls in love with her, and the narrative comment tells us that almost immediately he begins to idealize her. She is charming and beautiful anyway, but in his imagination he makes her taller and darker. He is aware that he does this, and even makes an effort to dismiss his fantasies of her before he actually sees her 'in order to prevent too painful a collision between what he dreamt of her and what she was'. What he actually discovers is that she is even 'more beautiful and strange than his dream of her'.

When Ralph is talking to Mary Datchet, he sounds perfectly rational on the subject of love:

It's only a story one makes up in one's mind about another person, and one knows all the time it isn't true. Of course one knows; why, one's always taking care not to destroy the illusion. One takes care not to see them too often, or to be alone with them for too long . . . It's a pleasant illusion . . .

(*Night and Day*, p.277)

Suffragettes released from Holloway Prison in 1912. Like them, Mary Datchet in Night and Day *campaigned for women's right to vote.*

But his understanding does not prevent him from continuing to indulge in daydreaming about Katherine. When he explains this 'school-boy' habit to Katherine herself, however, she tells him firmly: 'if you were to know me you would feel none of this . . . we don't know each other'. Her major reservation is that he has invented an imaginary Katherine and now 'can't separate me from the person you've imagined me to be'. But later he remarks that she keeps forgetting her purse – the most commonplace of details – and Katherine is shaken:

> She was capable of forgetting things. He saw that. But what more did he see? Was he not looking at something she had never shown to anybody? Was it not something so profound that the notion of his seeing it almost shocked her?
>
> (*Night and Day*, p.347)

There are no answers to these questions, just the sense that perhaps Ralph has come to know her better than she thought. Significantly enough, words are not adequate for framing the thoughts that she wants to articulate, so she gazes at him in silence 'with a look that seemed to ask what she could not put into words'. The difficulty of communication, and the impossibility of ever really knowing what another person is like, are developed in more interesting ways in Woolf's later novels.

Katherine is the granddaughter of a famous Victorian poet, Richard Allardyce, and her mother is engaged in writing his biography. It is destined never to be completed because although she has a wealth of material she is incapable of organizing it. Some of the subjects she addresses are important, others trivial. She writes:

> . . . twenty pages on her grandfather's taste in hats, an essay upon contemporary China, a long account of a summer day's expedition into the country, when they had missed their train, together with fragmentary visions of all sorts of famous men and women . . .
>
> (*Night and Day*, p.38)

All these things may have some reference to Richard Allardyce, but they seem to have been written more because they interest Mrs Hilbery, the poet's daughter. Lives seem to extend in all directions, and the desire to be all-inclusive means that Mrs Hilbery's biography is destined to remain muddled and incomplete.

Jacob's Room

It was in *Jacob's Room* that Woolf really began to experiment. One of the themes of *Night and Day* becomes the central idea: the impossibility of knowing another human being. The room of the title is the space into which other characters project their ideas of what Jacob is like. In July 1922 Woolf wrote in her diary: 'Leonard read through *Jacob's Room*. He thinks it is my best work . . . he thinks it unlike any other novel; he says that the people are ghosts'. Leonard's summing up of her characters as 'ghosts' is more likely to have been a compliment than a criticism, because Jacob is intended to be elusive.

The Somme, 1916. Jacob Flanders, as his name suggests, is destined to die during the First World War, in Jacob's Room.

43

Sometimes when we read a novel, we have the impression that the hero or heroine is real, we imagine what they might say or do, and long to know what happens to them after the end of the book. However, that is not the kind of characterization Woolf was aiming for.

Jacob is a small boy at the beginning, but he is not present in the opening pages. 'Where is that tiresome boy?' his mother asks, and the sea shore echoes with his brother's cry: 'Ja-cob! Ja-cob!' At the end of the book his friend Bonamy is in Jacob's bedroom sorting through his papers – because Jacob is gone, killed in the First World War. His surname – Flanders – suggests that this will be his fate, for countless young men lost their lives on Flanders Fields during the Great War. Jacob's absence at the start and end of the novel only underlines his elusiveness, and we are left wondering what he is really like.

Jacob's Room explores the way in which different people perceive the central character. Mrs Norman sits opposite him in a railway carriage, and initially sees him as a threat.

Mrs Norman, travelling on a train, thinks Jacob looks threatening when he enters her carriage. 'She would throw the scent bottle with her right hand, she decided, and tug the communication cord with her left.' She might be 50 years old and have a son at college herself, but she knows men are dangerous. Before her journey is over, however, she has revised her opinion and wishes to offer him her newspaper, in spite of the fact that they have not spoken, and Jacob seems quite unconscious of her presence. The narrative comment tells us:

> Nobody sees anyone as he is, let alone an elderly lady sitting opposite a strange young man in a railway carriage. They see a whole – they see all sorts of things – they see themselves . . .

(Jacob's Room, p.28)

This is Woolf's point. In her opinion, we never really know other people, we simply 'make up stories' about them, as Ralph did with Katherine in *Night and Day*. While Jacob is away in Greece, Fanny, who is in love with him, goes to the British Museum to gaze at a statue which reminds her of him:

> . . . keeping her eyes downcast until she was alongside of the battered Ulysses, she opened them and got a fresh shock of Jacob's presence, enough to last her half a day.

(Jacob's Room, p.166)

What she sees is her idea of Jacob, it has little reference to Jacob himself. Similarly, Mrs Jarvis reads one of Jacob's letters to his mother, and comments 'Jacob's letters are so like him' – though we as readers of the novel are aware that Jacob has told his mother nothing of what he is doing in Paris. We understand that his letter is 'like' him only in that it gives nothing away.

Readers put together conflicting impressions that characters in the novel have of Jacob, but it is not Woolf's intention that we should arrive at any real conclusion. There are very few passages which give us his own thoughts, and the narrator's knowledge seems as limited as that of the characters in the book: 'whether this is the right interpretation of Jacob's gloom . . . it is impossible to say'. Often an empty room is described. When Jacob is at Cambridge University his rooms were: 'in Neville's Court; at the top; so that reaching his door one went in a little out of breath; but he wasn't there'. Jacob escapes, because Woolf wanted to show the elusiveness and complexity of human character.

Mrs Dalloway

In *Mrs Dalloway* Woolf found a perfect form and structure for her subject. The events take place during one day and evening, leading up to Mrs Dalloway's party. Throughout the book, the famous clock of Big Ben chimes the hours: 'first a warning, musical, then the hour, irrevocable' (p.6). Woolf's working title for the book was 'The Hours', and undoubtedly the steady chiming of the clock, continually reminding us of objective time – the present moment, the time that is the same for all the characters in the novel – acts as an anchor and a major structuring device throughout the work.

This is important, for it establishes a plane of reality about which there is common agreement. It has to be firmly established within the novel as a kind of checkpoint, because Woolf was concerned to show another kind of reality, that of subjective time, and in particular, memory. Mrs Dalloway thinks back to her youth, before her marriage, to the trees at Bourton. Septimus Smith, who has less control over his memories, sees and hears a dead man coming towards him: Evans, who was killed during the war. As Septimus sits in a London park, his wife asks him the time:

> 'I will tell you the time,' said Septimus, very slowly, very drowsily, smiling mysteriously at the dead man in the grey suit. As he sat smiling, the quarter struck – the quarter to twelve.
>
> (*Mrs Dalloway*, p.64)

Thus in Septimus we are shown an extreme example of something which we all experience up to a point: co-existence in both subjective and objective time. While Big Ben strikes, his body and at least part of his mind are aware of the present moment. But the disturbed part of

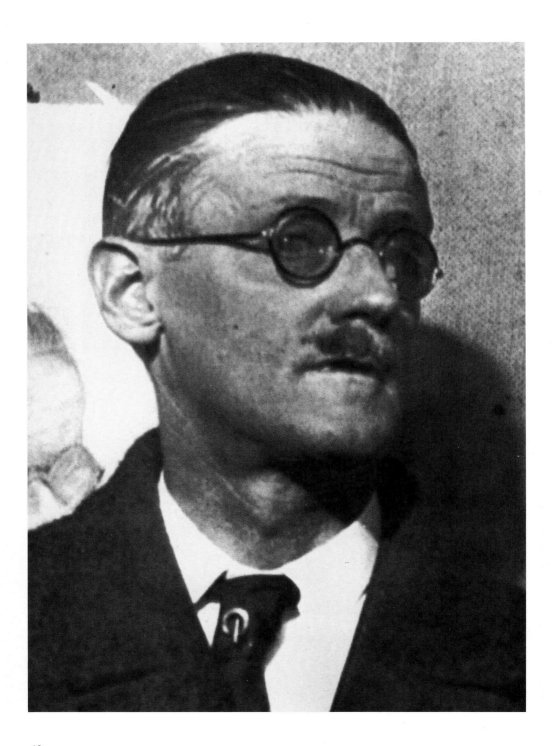

his mind has gone back several years and superimposes itself on the present. What his memory shows him is equally real.

Woolf felt that this thinking back to the past while the action of the novel is confined to less than twenty-four hours was a major discovery. In June 1923 she wrote in her diary:

> . . . the design is so queer and masterful. I'm always having to wrench my substance to fit it. The design is certainly original, and interests me hugely . . .

By August she had the design even more clearly in mind:

> I should say a great deal about 'The Hours', and my discovery; how I dig out beautiful caves behind my characters; I think that gives them exactly what I want; humanity, humour, depth. The idea is that the caves shall connect, and each comes to light at the present moment.

The major 'caves' are those of Septimus Smith and Clarissa Dalloway. 'I adumbrate here a study of insanity and suicide' Woolf wrote, 'the world seen by the sane and the insane'. Clarissa is sane, Septimus insane, and the latter commits suicide. The two never meet; Clarissa hears of his death only at the end of the novel – though even then she knows nothing of his name or circumstances.

Two characters could not be more different. Septimus volunteered for, and survived, the First World War; he married an Italian girl; he is thirty, male and working class. Clarissa is in her fifties, a society hostess – the Prime Minister is a guest at her party. But the movement of these two through the novel is another of the pivots around which the work is structured. However diverse they may seem, they are linked through imagery and motif. Often their thoughts echo each other's, which suggests that their perceptions of the world around them are not so different: there is, then, a connection between the sane and the insane. One of the refrains which runs repeatedly through Clarissa's mind is: 'Fear no more the heat o' the sun', a line from a song in Shakespeare's *Cymbeline*. Septimus does not repeat this precisely, but

Opposite *James Joyce, perhaps the most innovative writer of the modernist era. Like* Mrs Dalloway, *his famous novel* Ulysses *combines the action of twenty-four hours with flashbacks to the past. Joyce's novel was published three years earlier.*

Mrs Dalloway, a society hostess, would have presided over glittering dinner parties like this one.

he often thinks 'still, the sun was hot', and even before his suicide: 'Life was good, the sun hot'.

Nowhere in the novel does a narrator's voice draw our attention to such connections. Similarities are woven into the text, and the reader must make the links and draw his or her own conclusions about their significance. The closer we look, the more similarities we find. Clarissa is described as 'very white', with a face 'beaked like a bird's'. Septimus is 'pale-faced, beak-nosed'. Clarissa chooses flowers for her party, 'how fresh . . . the roses looked; and dark and prim the red carnations, holding their heads up'. For Septimus 'red flowers grew through his flesh, their stiff leaves mottled by his head', and he reminds himself that 'thick red roses' grow on his bedroom wall.

Motifs like these direct us to a more fundamental link, which suggests that sanity and insanity are simply two points on the same continuum, one more extreme than the other. Septimus has committed the 'crime' of not feeling (see above, 'Death and Madness'). First when Evans was killed, later when he became engaged: 'he could not feel'. The phrase is repeated relentlessly – six times in the space of two pages, which gives us the sense of madness and obsession as we read (*Mrs Dalloway*, p.78-9). It is his ability to detach himself from normal emotions which leads him to the terrifying possibility that 'the world itself is without meaning'.

Mrs Dalloway has encountered nothing so traumatic, and yet like Septimus she too has had a fear of feeling intense emotion: so much so that she refused Peter Walsh's proposal, and married Richard Dalloway instead:

> For in marriage a little licence, a little independence there must be between people living together day in day out in the same house; which Richard gave her and she him. (Where was he this morning, for instance? Some committee, she never asked what.) But with Peter everything had to be shared; everything gone into. And it was intolerable.

(*Mrs Dalloway*, p.9)

Clarissa chose against passion and excitement, and the result, as she enters her house with the flowers for her party, is that she: 'felt like a nun who has left the world'. The nun image is repeated several times. She sleeps alone, and cannot dispel the sense of: 'a virginity preserved through childbirth'. Such imagery, reinforcing her self-imposed isolation, suggests that had she been exposed to strong emotion, she too might have become insane. Equally, by protecting herself from passion, as Septimus mentally detached himself from horror, she has become isolated and disengaged, just as Septimus has become alienated.

For this reason, it is Clarissa who has an intuitive understanding of Septimus's reasons, when, at her party, she hears that a young man has killed himself. Her first thought is a selfish one, she does not want to have her feelings disturbed: 'Oh! thought Clarissa, in the middle of my party here's death, she thought' and she leaves the social gathering and goes into a little room to be alone. This sums up precisely her need for isolation, her need to protect herself from strong emotion: 'What business had the Bradshaws to talk of death at her party?'

Mrs Dalloway knows none of the details of Septimus's death, but as she begins to think about it, in her imagination she reconstructs his suicide:

> He had thrown himself from a window. Up had flashed the ground; through him, blundering, bruising, went the rusty spikes. There he lay with a thud, thud, thud in his brain, and then a suffocation of blackness. So she saw it.

(*Mrs Dalloway*, p.163)

The Serpentine lake in Hyde Park, London. Mrs Dalloway connects Septimus' suicide with a moment when she threw a shilling into the Serpentine.

There follows the major question: 'But why had he done it?' Searching in her own experience for a parallel, she can only think that she once threw a shilling into the Serpentine:

> . . . a thing there was that mattered; a thing, wreathed about with chatter, defaced, obscured in her own life, let drop every day in corruption, lies, chatter. This he had preserved. Death was defiance, Death was an attempt to communicate.

> (*Mrs Dalloway*, p.163)

Clarissa has no way of knowing whether her intuition is right, but the reader remembers that Septimus jumped in order to avoid talking to Dr Holmes – in order to

avoid false communication with a man unable to understand. And paradoxically by throwing his life away, Septimus has communicated with the unlikely figure of a woman he has never met. He jumped to preserve his inner self, his integrity.

Clarissa considers her own life and 'an awful fear' in the depths of her heart. She walks to the window (as

Septimus did before he jumped) and sees an old lady in the room opposite 'quietly going to bed alone' – as Septimus did metaphorically, and as Clarissa will eventually. 'She felt somehow very like him – the young man who had killed himself', and then, restored by her moments of isolation and withdrawal into herself, 'she came in from the little room', and rejoined her party.

A party is a social gathering, and yet Woolf suggests that in an event designed for people to meet and talk, there is little real communication. Instead, she shows that communication can be wordless and instinctive – yet one has no way of checking the accuracy of one's insights.

Early in the novel, Clarissa, Septimus and a number of other characters who do not reappear, see an impressive motor car in a London street: 'Was it the Prince of Wales's, the Queen's, the Prime Minister's? Whose face was it? Nobody knew.' Similarly a skywriting aeroplane flies overhead. Here again is an objective reality, about which there should be common agreement. But each observer perceives the writing differently: '"Blaxo", said Mrs Coates, "Kreemo" murmured Mrs Bletchley. "It's toffee" Mr Bowley thinks, while the nursemaid spells out "K . . . P . . ."'.

When Septimus looks at the car, he sees a pattern on the blinds drawn at the windows and it seems to him 'as if some horror had come almost to the surface and was about to burst into flames'. When Clarissa sees it she is certain that it contains the Queen or Prime Minister; but the narrative comment, which may or may not echo her thoughts (see page 68, 'Interior monologue'), uses language similar to Septimus's thoughts. As the car drives away, it 'burnt its way through . . . to blaze among candelabras'. Their perceptions could not be more different, yet through the language they are linked, in preparation for the 'caves' which connect at the end.

The contrast between different perceptions is used throughout as another major structuring device. Sometimes it is humorous, as when different people read the same words differently, but even then there are sinister implications about the subjectivity of response. A more ironic example is that of Peter Walsh observing the ambulance which whisks away Septimus's dead or dying body:

Opposite *In* Mrs Dalloway, *a number of characters see an impressive car in a London street, but each one thinks something different about it:* 'Was it the Prince of Wales's, the Queen's, the Prime Minister's?'

55

One of the triumphs of civilization, Peter Walsh thought. It is one of the triumphs of civilization, as the light high bell of the ambulance sounded. Swiftly, cleanly, the ambulance sped to the hospital . . . the efficiency, the communal spirit of London.

(*Mrs Dalloway*, p.134)

In one way he is right, but equally 'civilization' was responsible for the war which sent Septimus mad, and for providing doctors like Holmes and Bradshaw:

'It is one of the triumphs of civilization,' Peter Walsh thinks in Mrs Dalloway, *when he sees the ambulance that is taking away Septimus' body.*

. . . men who made ten thousand a year and talked of proportion; who differed on their verdicts (for Holmes said one thing, Bradshaw another), yet judges they were; who . . . saw nothing clear, yet ruled, yet inflicted.

(*Mrs Dalloway* p.131)

Society promotes only the most superficial kind of communication, obscuring real connections and substituting false ones.

To the Lighthouse

Woolf is known as an experimental novelist and an innovator partly because she never repeated a form, searching instead for an appropriate method of presenting her material in each new work. She saw the world and our experience of it as essentially fragmentary, and this was one of the things she sought to express in her fiction. At the same time she was always concerned to make sense of the fragments, to arrange them into some kind of artistic coherence; as Lily Briscoe thinks: 'in the midst of chaos there was shape'. It is her job as a painter, and Woolf's as a writer, to find and express that shape. 'Beautiful and bright it should be on the surface' Lily thinks:

> . . . feathery and evanescent, one colour melting into another like the colours on a butterfly's wing; but beneath the fabric must be clamped together with bolts of iron. It was to be a thing you could ruffle with your breath; and a thing you could not dislodge with a team of horses.

> (*To the Lighthouse*, p.159)

Lily's painting of Mrs Ramsay and her son James represents them as a triangular purple shape, dividing her canvas into three parts. The novel itself has a three-part structure. 'The Window', a long first section, deals with the events of one afternoon and evening, when a trip to the lighthouse is planned for the next day. The short central section, by contrast, covers ten years during which Mrs Ramsay dies; Prue, one of her daughters, marries and dies during childbirth; the First World War takes place and Andrew, a son, dies in action. The last section, 'The Lighthouse' shows some of the family – Mr Ramsay, James and Cam, with Mr Bankes and Lily Briscoe – all reassembled at the house. The action covers part of one day, and the lighthouse is finally reached.

These three parts are the 'bolts of iron', reinforced not only by Lily's painting, but by the flashes of light from the lighthouse: 'first two quick strokes and then one long steady stroke'. In 'The Window' Mrs Ramsay looks out 'to meet that stroke of the lighthouse, the long steady stroke, the last of the three, which was her stroke'.

This is an important image in the book, for though in one sense the lighthouse has no one single meaning – it is intended to be both real, and infinitely suggestive – symbolically it has a great deal in common with Mrs Ramsay. It is there to communicate, to keep ships off rocks and out of danger. One of Mrs Ramsay's main roles in life is to care for her eight children, her husband, their guests. She gives, understands their needs, communicates. Like the lighthouse, however, she is also difficult to reach. She has an isolated inner self which even her husband seems not to suspect:

> All the being and doing evaporated; and one [i.e. Mrs Ramsay] shrunk, with a sense of solemnity, to being oneself, a wedge-shaped core of darkness, something invisible to others . . . this core of darkness could go anywhere, for no one saw it.

(To the Lighthouse, p.61)

And yet Lily, the artist, struggling with the taunts of Charles Tansley – 'women can't paint, women can't write' – intuitively sees Mrs Ramsay as a purplish triangular shadow. Working on her painting after Mrs Ramsay's death, and thinking of her love (as well as her irritation) for her, Lily sees someone inside the house move and 'an odd triangular shadow' is thrown across the step. This shadow corresponds to Mrs Ramsay's private image of herself, and though Lily has no knowledge of this, it helps her to complete her painting. It is another example of non-verbal communication, one person understanding something about another, as Clarissa did with Septimus. However, as in *Mrs Dalloway,* since Mrs Ramsay is dead, Lily has no confirmation of the accuracy of her perception.

Mrs Ramsay is the main anchor to which the narrative keeps returning. Much of the first section is seen from her point of view, and when we follow other characters' thoughts, it is most often to her that they turn.

Mr and Mrs Ramsay complement each other. He is a man who 'had made a definite contribution to philosophy' in a book written when he was twenty-five. Since then his work has been mainly 'amplification, repetition'. His mind may be 'splendid', but it runs in straight lines and abstractions. If thought could be

Opposite *The artist Lily Briscoe in the 1983 BBC adaptation of* To the Lighthouse.

divided up into letters of the alphabet, Mr Ramsay has reached 'Q'; 'very few people in the whole of England ever reach Q'. But he is insecure because 'R' is beyond him: 'How many men in a thousand million, he asked himself, reach Z after all?' Mr Ramsay feels himself to be a failure, and requires continual reassurance from his wife that he is a genius. James, his youngest son, standing between his mother's knees, feels the demands his father makes on her:

Opposite *Vanessa Bell in 1913. Like Lily Briscoe, she was an artist.*

Virginia's father, Leslie Stephen, in academic robes. Woolf partly based Mr Ramsay in To the Lighthouse *on him.*

James Ramsay with his mother, in the BBC production of To the Lighthouse.

James felt all her strength flare up to be drenched by the beak of brass, the arid scimitar of the male, which smote and smote again demanding sympathy.

(*To the Lighthouse*, p.39)

Mrs Ramsay is a more complex character than her husband. Lily, dwelling on her memory, thinks 'one wanted fifty pairs of eyes to see with . . . Fifty pairs of eyes were not enough to get round that one woman'. She is not a modern woman. Her daughters, Prue, Nancy and Rose:

> . . . could sport with infidel ideas which they had brewed for themselves of a life different from hers . . . a wilder life, not always taking care of some man or other.

> (*To the Lighthouse*, p.12)

Clearly they have something in common with Vanessa and Virginia, and like Julia Stephen, Mrs Ramsay is not content to care for her own family, but visits 'this widow, or that struggling wife in person', notebook and pencil in hand, trying to do something about poverty.

Mrs Ramsay is not only good and beautiful, she is also a matchmaker and to some extent a meddler: Lily must marry William Bankes (she doesn't), and she promotes the marriage of Paul Rayley and Minta Doyle – which we later learn was unsuccessful.

Her real talent, however, lies in her attempts to create a sense of unity and wholeness, to make of fleeting moments something permanent. What Woolf does with her novel, and Lily with her painting – ordering fragments and revealing unity, a pattern, a structure – Mrs Ramsay attempts with her family and guests. In a sense she too is an artist. At dinner she feels at first a sense of disappointment:

> Nothing seemed to have merged. They all sat separate. And the whole of the effort of merging and flowing and creating rested on her. Again she felt, as a fact without hostility, the sterility of men, for if she did not do it, nobody would do it.

> (*To the Lighthouse*, p.79)

As if collecting fragments, she works at mellowing William Bankes and drawing Charles Tansley into her charmed circle. Lily remains detached, aware of her efforts, and wonders what would happen if 'one were not nice to that young man there'. But she too is drawn

Jasper on the beach in Cornwall, from the BBC version of To the Lighthouse. *The novel was partly inspired by Woolf's memories of childhood holidays in St Ives.*

in, answering Mrs Ramsay's mute appeal for help, communicated not by words but by a glance. She responds to Mrs Ramsay's unspoken pressure and is pleasant to Tansley, despising her own weakness in complying as she does so:

> She had done the usual trick – been nice. She would never know him. Human relations were all like that, she thought, and the worst . . . were between men and women. Inevitably these were extremely insincere.

(*To the Lighthouse*, p.86-7)

Characteristically, Woolf's subject here is the difficulty of knowing another human being.

When the candles are lit, momentarily Mrs Ramsay achieves her object, for the candlelight draws the faces round the table together, shuts out the night and establishes the party as a kind of island:

> Some change at once went through them all, as if this had really happened, and they were all conscious of making a party together.
>
> (*To the Lighthouse*, p.91)

Such moments of unity are two-sided, for Woolf sets them against a larger canvas of time and nature which change and destroy.

The effects of time are shown most clearly in the short central 'Time Passes' section. The house remains empty, the family do not return, and without human effort to hold back the destructive forces of nature, it begins to fall into ruins. Shabby and ramshackle in the opening part, it deteriorates almost beyond repair:

> . . . the house was deserted. It was left like a shell on a sandhill to fill with dry soft grains now that life had left it. The long night seemed to have set in . . . The saucepan had rusted and the mat decayed. Toads had nosed their way in . . . the swallows had nested in the drawing room.
>
> (*To the Lighthouse*, p.128)

The descriptions of the decaying house are also metaphors for the destruction of Europe during the First World War. In short parenthetical statements interposed within descriptions of the house, we learn a number of objective facts:

> (A shell exploded. Twenty or thirty young men were blown up in France, among them Andrew Ramsay, whose death, mercifully, was instantaneous.)
>
> (*To the Lighthouse*, p.124)

We learn of the deaths of Mrs Ramsay and Prue in the

Prue Ramsay in the BBC's To the Lighthouse. *In the short central section of the novel, we learn that Prue has died in childbirth.*

same way (see p.16 'Death and Madness'. Private histories and world history are not being belittled, but placed in a wider context. People will always die, wars have always and will continue to be fought – Woolf's canvas goes beyond the early history of the twentieth century. Man's instinct is to build houses or civilizations – which, if left unattended, will decay. But this is not a pessimistic vision, rather a recognition of things as they are, and also a tribute to human optimism and endeavour. In the house:

> . . . had come that moment, that hesitation when dawn trembles and night passes, when if a feather alight in the scale it will be weighed down. One feather, and the house, sinking, falling, would have turned and pitched downwards to the depths of darkness.

> (*To the Lighthouse*, p.129)

Nancy in the BBC adaptation of To the Lighthouse.

'If' the feather had fallen – but it does not: 'there was a force working; something not highly conscious . . .' In the persons of Mrs McNab and Mrs Bast, the women from the village employed as cleaners to turn the balance and exert control over nature, Woolf demonstrates her belief that 'the whole world is a work of art; that we are parts of the work of art'. They are uneducated women, 'not highly conscious' – unlike Mrs Ramsay presiding over her party, or Lily painting – but their role is comparable, for they too are preserving and restoring.

Set in this wide context of eternal struggle with the environment, the achievement is qualified. Some day, inevitably, the balance will tip the other way. Equally, it can be tipped back. That 'this cannot last' is inevitable, and Mrs Ramsay, as well as Woolf, is aware of the fact.

Interior monologue, style and syntax

'Stream of consciousness' is a term often used to describe a technique used by writers like Woolf, Joyce and Proust, contemporaries who all attempted to capture in their writing the multiplicity of the mind at work. It is not quite accurate, however, for not only is it impossible to capture every nuance of consciousness on paper, it would also be very boring indeed to read. We are capable of thinking on many different levels at the same time – some thoughts may be important, some trivial; often our thoughts are repetitive. The writer would not wish to reproduce all this, even if it could be done. In writing, one word must follow the next; it is not possible to write several things simultaneously, nor would it be possible to read them. So Woolf creates an impression, gives an artistic representation of the flow of thought, and the term 'interior monologue' best describes the result. Her writing is not random and all-inclusive; it may give this impression, but in fact it is selective.

While Mrs Ramsay is engaged in thinking about marriage, life and children, for example, she also has something else on her mind:

Marriage needed – oh all sorts of qualities (the bill for the greenhouse roof would be fifty pounds); one – she need not name it – *that* was essential.

(*To the Lighthouse*, p.59)

Opposite Mr Ramsay, philosopher and father of eight children, in the BBC production of To the Lighthouse.

The greenhouse roof is a practical worry. It may seem like a random thought, but financial considerations can be as important in day to day married life as philosophical ideas. The greenhouse intrudes, always in brackets, several times: a reminder to Mrs Ramsay and the reader of an objective reality, a problem to be dealt with – comically not unconnected with larger questions of destruction and preservation.

Woolf often uses long winding sentences to capture conflicting and associative thoughts. At the dinner party, for example, at first 'Everything seemed possible. Everything seemed right.' Two short statements present a moment of rest, 'seemed' is conditional, but the overall sense is one of certainty. They are followed, however, by a very long sentence:

> Just now (but this cannot last, she thought, dissociating herself from the moment while they were all talking about books) just now she had reached security; she hovered like a hawk suspended; like a flag floated in an element of joy which filled every nerve of her body fully and sweetly, not noisily, solemnly rather, for it arose, she thought, looking at them all eating there, from husband and children and friends; all of which rising in this profound stillness (she was helping William Bankes to one very small piece more and peered into the depths of the earthenware pot) seemed now for no special reason to stay there like smoke, like a fume rising upwards, holding them safe together.

(*To the Lighthouse*, p.97)

As she thinks 'just now' Mrs Ramsay's mind almost simultaneously recognizes the opposite, '(but this cannot last . . .)'. Even so, at this particular moment, security is uppermost. The ebb and flow of thought is represented in rhythmical, poetic prose, the sentence circles back on itself, defining and redefining with a series of images: 'like a hawk', 'like a flag'. Such images represent the way Mrs Ramsay feels; perhaps she actually thinks those words, but equally they could simply be a translation into language of a sense of well-being – whichever it is, Woolf *represents* them as part of Mrs Ramsay's interior monologue. The same scene could have been

Opposite *James Ramsay, who thinks his mother is '...ten thousand times better in every way' than his father.*

presented like this: 'Mrs Ramsay sat at the table and looked round at her family and guests. This is perfect she thought, but at the same time she was aware that though she would always remember this moment, she couldn't count on the others feeling or remembering it in the same way.' Comparing the flatness of that with Woolf's writing shows how interested she was in trying to capture nuances of consciousness.

Rhythmically, the sentence winds on, punctuated by semi-colons and commas, incorporating her actions – serving a second helping to Mr Bankes – and finally comes to rest with an image of smoke 'holding them all together'.

Short sentences followed by long winding ones are characteristic of Woolf's style. She frequently makes use of parentheses (information given in brackets) to give the impression of simultaneous thoughts, or actions, which may be unconnected with the interior monologue.

Questions are also typical of her style. Lily, for example, asks herself:

> . . . was she crying for Mrs Ramsay, without being aware of her own unhappiness? . . . What was it then? What did it mean? Could things thrust their hands up and grip one; could the blade cut; the fist grasp? Was there no safety? No learning by heart of the ways of the world? No guide, no shelter, but all was miracle, and leaping from the pinnacle of a tower into the air? Could it be, even for elderly people, that this was life? – startling, unexpected, unknown?

(*To the Lighthouse*, p.166-7)

Characteristically too, the text offers us no definitive answers. Searching and questioning are present throughout *To the Lighthouse* and Woolf's fiction as a whole. The effort to understand what life is about is seen as important in itself, and Woolf's honesty prevents her from offering us trite or simple answers. Each apparently definitive statement is countered by its opposite. Thus Lily's thought '"you" and "I" and "she" pass and vanish; nothing stays; all changes; but not words, not paint' is countered by her knowledge that her painting is likely to be put in an attic, or rolled up and flung under a sofa.

Opposite *Lily Briscoe's question: 'What did it mean?' is typical of the sense of searching for an answer that runs throughout* To the Lighthouse.

Later novels

Orlando followed *To the Lighthouse*. It is more light-hearted, a fictional biography following its central character from his youth in Elizabethan England, through his remarkable transformation into a woman in the eighteenth century, and charting *her* progress up to the moment in the twentieth when Woolf was writing. *Orlando* was written as a tribute to Vita Sackville-West, a friend of Woolf's with whom she was more than half in love. The house in the novel is based on the Sackville-Wests' family home, Knole, in Kent, and in one sense *Orlando* is a history of the family. It is also a history of English literature, for various styles characteristic of each century are parodied.

In her diary Woolf described the writing of it as 'a writer's holiday'. 'It has to be half-laughing, half-serious' she wrote, 'with great splashes of exaggeration'. This is precisely what she achieved. Her tone is comic and mocking, yet she addresses her usual subjects: the difficulties of writing, the difficulty of knowing, let alone describing, another human being. In the second chapter the biographer (of this fictional character Orlando) says:

> . . . documents, both private and historical, have made it possible to fulfil the first duty of a biographer, which is to plod, without looking to left or right, in the indelible footprints of the truth.

> (*Orlando*, p.41)

Clearly this is Woolf's last priority. She mistrusted so-called objective facts, and was also aware that they would make dull reading. Later, with mock horror, the narrator/biographer is obliged to 'speculate, to surmise, and even to use the imagination!' in the absence of documentary evidence covering a certain period of Orlando's life. Woolf may be weaving an entertaining and elaborate joke, but her certain knowledge that dates and places tell us nothing that we want to know about a character (whether real or invented) never wavers.

Orlando becomes a woman half way through the book, an event used to discuss the difference between men's and women's experience of life. As a woman in the eighteenth century Orlando finds her elaborate clothing both pleasing and constricting – occasionally she

Opposite *Knole, near Sevenoaks in Kent, family home of the Sackville-Wests. Vita Sackville-West was a close friend of Woolf's, and* Orlando *was partly based on her family.*

75

Men's and women's clothes in the eighteenth century. Orlando changes sex to become a woman in the eighteenth century, but finding the elaborate clothes restricting, she sometimes dresses as a man.

disregards it in favour of men's. Freedom from constriction also means freedom to roam the streets at night unmolested. She meets a group of prostitutes, lively and companionable once they realize she is actually a woman. The companionship and insight into their lives would normally have been unavailable to her: as a woman of her social standing their paths would not have crossed; equally, had she been a man, the exchange would have been purely professional.

Woolf, always sharply aware of inequalities between men and women, wanted to promote better understanding, and, ultimately, less rigid definitions of masculinity and femininity.

The Waves is often considered to be Woolf's most difficult and experimental work. There is a sense in which it continues her idea of androgeny – striving for a balance of male and female qualities within one human being – which was playfully expressed in *Orlando*, and considered differently in *A Room of One's Own* (see page 82). The six characters: Susan, Jinny, Rhoda, Neville, Louis and Bernard, are separate individuals with sharply defined characteristics. Susan longs for home and family when she is a child at school; she is an 'earth-mother' who marries and brings up her children in the country. Jinny could not be more different: a mistress rather than a wife, glittering and confident. Rhoda is insecure and fearful, in some ways she corresponds to Louis among the male characters, while Neville is an intellectual, impatient with Bernard, who is always weaving stories, who identifies with the authors and characters of whatever he is reading at the time.

Separate individuals though they are, they are also 'six petals of one flower', 'six slices of one cake' and six instruments making up an orchestra. They have also been linked through their common love for Percival, a character who never actually appears in the novel other than in their thoughts. Only Bernard speaks in the final section recapitulating his life and his memories of the others. He finds it hard to distinguish himself from them:

> Now I ask, 'Who am I?' I have been talking of Bernard, Neville, Jinny, Susan, Rhoda and Louis. Am I all of them? Am I one and distinct? I do not know . . . I cannot find any obstacle separating us . . . Here on my brow is the blow I got when Percival fell. Here on the nape of my neck is the kiss Jinny gave Louis. My eyes fill with Susan's tears.
>
> (*The Waves*, p.195)

Together they make up aspects of one character, a complex identity balanced between male and female experience. In so far as Bernard knows the others, they really are inside his head – an idea Woolf began to develop as early as *Mrs Dalloway*, with Clarissa's feeling of being laid out like a mist between people she knew best.

There is no dialogue – no exchange between the characters – as we usually understand it in *The Waves*. Instead, they each have monologues, describing their situation, their thoughts about the others, and they speak in turn at various stages of their lives, from childhood to late middle or old age. These sections are divided by passages of natural description: the position of the sun in the sky, the sea, birds, snails, which both reflect and predict their states of mind.

After reaching her most extreme 'experiment' in *The Waves*, Woolf did something quite different with *The Years*. It is much more conventional than anything she had written since *Night and Day*, her second novel. When it first came out it sold better than any of her previous novels, perhaps because it was more immediately accessible. *The Years* follows three generations of the Pargiter family, from 1880 to the 'Present Day' – Eleanor, Colonel Pargiter's eldest daughter, is over seventy in the final part of the novel. Although it is a family chronicle, not all details are filled in: the second part jumps eleven years to 1891, part three is set in 1907, and so on. Woolf tries, not always successfully, to give a more conventional historical background to this work, but her usual concerns are ever present. Maggie thinks:

Leonard Woolf, Clive and Julian Bell, Virginia Woolf, Quentin Bell and Duncan Grant at Charleston Farm in Sussex, in 1930. Woolf was writing The Waves *at this time.*

Am I that, or am I this? Are we one, or are we separate
. . . 'What's "I"? . . . "I" . . .' She stopped. She did not
know what she meant. She was talking nonsense.

(The Years, p.108)

Between the Acts was Woolf's last novel, left unrevised
after her suicide in 1941. It was written during the early
years of the Second World War (1939–45), a time of
intense anxiety for everyone. At the same time, Woolf
herself was battling with depression, and feared the
onset of another period of madness. For all this, *Between
the Acts* is an optimistic and even funny novel.

Like *Mrs Dalloway*, the action of *Between the Acts* takes
place during the course of one day. But in that basic

eighteen-hour structure, Woolf manages to sketch in English history from prehistoric times to the moment of writing; a survey of English literature from Chaucer to the Victorians, and the history of a particular family precisely located within their rural society.

Lucy Swithin and Bartholomew Oliver, elderly brother and sister, represent the late Victorian/early Edwardian past. Giles, Bartholomew's son, and his wife Isa, are the present generation, and their son George shows the family continuing into the future. The Oliver family live in Pointz Hall, a medium-sized English country manor house which presides over the village and villagers like a relic of the English feudal system.

The novel opens prosaically enough with a discussion of the site of a new cesspool: in itself a reminder of mortality and decay, and yet also of the continuation of the human race. Modern technology, in the form of an aeroplane, provides an overall picture of the way in which history has been written into the land:

Mr Oliver, of the Indian Civil Service, retired – said that the site they had chosen for the cesspool was, if he had heard right, on the Roman road. From an aeroplane, he said, you could still see, plainly marked, the scars made by the Britons; by the Romans; by the Elizabethan manor house; and by the plough, when they ploughed the hill to grow wheat in the Napoleonic wars.

(*Between the Acts*, p.7)

Economically, in one short paragraph, Woolf encompasses Britons, Romans, Elizabethans, Napoleonic wars, and, in the person of Mr Oliver himself, retired from the Indian Civil Service, a reminder of British Imperialism.

The action of the novel revolves around a pageant written by Miss La Trobe. It is really a literary journey through English history, performed by the villagers; but audience and actors are seen to be equally important. The pageant brings everyone together, the 'tick tick tick tick' of the gramophone needle seems sometimes 'to hold them together, tranced' and yet just as Mrs Ramsay was aware that the moment of unity could not last, Isa thinks: 'Dispersed are we . . . all is over. The wave has broken. Left us stranded . . . Single, separate on the shingle'.

Opposite *A late portrait of Virginia Woolf.*

4 A Room of One's Own

In 1928 Woolf was invited to give lectures at Newnham and Girton, the two women's colleges at Cambridge University, on women and fiction. She adapted and published them as *A Room of One's Own* in 1929.

Typically the book begins with the difficulties of the subject; it could be interpreted as:

> . . . women and what they are like, or it might mean women and the fiction that they write; or it might mean women and the fiction that is written about them.

> (*A Room of One's Own*, p.5)

Inevitably she addresses all of these, and shows that it is impossible to separate them. *A Room of One's Own* is witty and entertaining; Woolf's tone is light and she often creates the impression that she is writing as thoughts present themselves. In fact, the book is carefully ordered, every anecdote or seeming flight of fancy has a serious bearing on the questions raised about the inequalities between men and women.

The first part of the book describes a day spent in Cambridge, a university town and one of the oldest educational establishments in England. Woolf contrasts her visit to one of the old colleges – exclusively male establishments in those days – with a visit to 'Fernham', a fictional representation of Newnham, then about fifty years old, and new in comparison. She points out the discrepancies between the education, traditions,

Opposite *The beginning of an early draft of* A Room of One's Own, *found among Woolf's notes.*

A Room of ones Own.

But, you may say, we asked you to speak about
women & fiction: What has that got to do with
a room of ones own? I will explain. When you asked
me to speak about women & fiction it seemed simple
enough. A few . . . . .

But that on thinking over, the subject but at second
sight the words seem not so simple.
I sat down on the banks of a river & began to think
what the words meant. They might mean simply . .

And when I began to consider them in their last way I
saw almost that I should see of I considered women -
fiction in that way I should never come to any
conclusion except a few
saw that I should never come to any conclusion.
I should only Express an opinion - that one must
have money & a room of one own: that one must have 500 a year
But why did I come to hold that opinion? & a room with a
That is what I propose to tell you & since
I am only giving you an opinion, & not a conclusion,
I am going to let you see for yourselves how I came to
I am going to develop in your presence as fully
freely as I can the train of thought which led me to
think this. The only way when a subject is as
controversial & as complicated as this one appears is not

84

independence and cultural life of men, and the relatively impoverished existence of women.

As a woman unaccompanied by a (male) member of the university, she is refused admittance to the university library. She is spotted walking on a hallowed college lawn: 'I was a woman. This was the turf; there was the path. Only the Fellows and Scholars are allowed here; the gravel is the place for me'. She is a guest at a lunch party given at one of the men's colleges: wine flows, course follows course, college silver and college servants abound, inevitably generating a sense of well-being. But as she leaves:

> . . . gate after gate seemed to close with gentle finality behind me. Innumerable beadles were fitting innumerable keys into well-oiled locks; the treasure house was being made secure for another night.

(A Room of One's Own, p.14)

Opposite Woolf in *1928, when she visited Cambridge to give lectures on 'Women and Fiction.'*

Male students at Cambridge in 1926. The type of education they received was, Woolf complained, still largely closed to women.

A tea-party at Girton College, Cambridge. Woolf admired the openness of the women's colleges.

By contrast, the women's college lies 'wild and open'; instead of being sixteenth-century it is built of Victorian red brick; a girl 'raced across the grass – would no one stop her?' – no one does. Dinner at Fernham is nourishing but plain – there is water to drink instead of wine. Clearly the odds have been stacked against women, but Woolf refuses to be bitter, her attitude is that the bastions

of male privilege are, paradoxically, men's loss. The imagery she uses all reinforces this: locked gates, rules and regulations, in opposition to the openness of the women's college. This is summed up at the end of the first section when she says of her experience at the library, 'I thought how unpleasant it is to be locked out; and I thought how it is worse perhaps to be locked in'.

A woman in her study at Girton. Woolf suggested that the difference between men's and women's colleges could be an advantage.

Woolf was working on *To the Lighthouse* at the same time as *A Room of One's Own*, and similar attitudes are apparent in both works. In the second part of *A Room* she visits the British Museum library in search of ideas about 'women and fiction':

> . . . here I had come with a notebook and a pencil proposing to spend a morning reading, supposing that at the end of the morning I should have transferred truth to my notebook.
>
> (*A Room of One's Own*, p.27)

This is a deliberately naive pose. Truth is always elusive, and acknowledging the impossibility of the task before her she uses an image of male sterility which occurs in *To the Lighthouse* to express it: 'I should need claws of steel and beak of brass to even penetrate the husk'. Secure in her own attitudes, she pretends to be intimidated by the male student seated beside her in the library 'copying assiduously from a scientific manual' extracting, she is convinced, 'pure nuggets of the essential ore every ten minutes or so'. As her own researches lead her deeper into contradiction and confusion – Goethe honoured women, Mussolini despised them – she glances:

> . . . with envy at the reader next door who was making the neatest abstracts, headed often with an A or a B or a C, while my own notebook rioted with the wildest of contradictory jottings.
>
> (*A Room of One's Own*, p.30)

Opposite *Marian Evans, who wrote under the name George Eliot. Woolf pointed out in the lectures on 'Women and Fiction' that she, like many great women novelists, was childless.*

Knowledge neatly catalogued in such a way recalls Mr Ramsay who had reached 'Q'. Women may not have had the advantage of training in scholarly research that men have had, but as Woolf's whole essay shows, that does not mean they are illogical or incapable of coherent thought. The refusal to categorize is seen instead as a strength; openness is opposed to confined and limited thought.

History has been divisive for the sexes. What were our mothers doing over the centuries, Woolf asks, that they had no money with which to endow colleges for

their daughters' education? The answer is that they were bringing up children. As she points out, it is also worth considering that among successful women novelists of the nineteenth century, Jane Austen, George Eliot, Charlotte and Emily Brontë were all childless.

Men's superior educational opportunities and their financial independence are, in her opinion, the reason why these male preserves are guarded the more jealously – because women are seen as a threat. Her answer to the problem may seem trite: women need five hundred pounds a year (in those days enough to ensure independence) and a room of their own. Symbolically, 'five hundred a year stands for the power to contemplate, a lock on the door means the power to think for oneself'. If this were possible, women would no longer be angry at the fate of their sex, they would have equal opportunities for developing creative, artistic talent: for how can anyone write well when injustice is at the forefront of their minds? Woolf uses some examples from *Jane Eyre*, and comments:

> . . . it is clear that anger was tampering with the integrity of Charlotte Brontë the novelist. She left her story, to which her entire devotion was due, to attend to some personal grievance. She remembered that she had been starved of her proper due of experience – she had been made to stagnate in a parsonage when she wanted to wander free over the world.
>
> (*A Room of One's Own*, p.70)

Whether one agrees with this or not, it leads Woolf into a development of her ideas about androgeny. She imagines:

> . . . a plan of the soul so that in each of us two powers preside, one male, one female; and in the man's brain the man predominates over the woman, and in the woman's brain the woman predominates over the man. The normal and comfortable state of being is when the two live in harmony together.
>
> (*A Room of One's Own*, p.93)

Woolf is not suggesting that a man's mind should have any special sympathy with a woman's, or vice versa,

Opposite *As Woolf pointed out, like George Eliot, Charlotte Brontë had no children. Charlotte died during pregnancy.*

instead she imagines human beings achieving *unconsciousness* of their sex, for only then is art possible:

> . . . it is fatal for anyone who writes to think of their sex. It is fatal to be a man or woman pure and simple, one must be womanly-manly or man-womanly . . .

– this is similar to Bernard's state at the end of *The Waves*, while it is an inevitable condition for Orlando:

> It is fatal for a woman to lay the least stress on any grievance; to plead even with justice any cause; in any way to speak consciously as a woman. And fatal is no figure of speech; for anything written with that conscious bias is doomed to death. It ceases to be fertilized . . . it cannot grow in the minds of others.
>
> (*A Room of One's Own*, p.99)

Woolf is not writing as a feminist here, she is writing as an artist on the subject of fiction, envisaging the artist's state of mind in which feminism is redundant, unnecessary. A true work of art should, in her opinion, transcend barriers of sex, and play no part in struggles for power or domination.

Three Guineas

Three Guineas was written during the Spanish Civil War (1936–39) as storm clouds gathered over Europe. It was published in 1938, the year before the Second World War began. This context is important, for the book takes the form of a letter addressed to a man who has written to Woolf, asking: 'How in your opinion are we to prevent war?' Woolf attempts to answer – even though she feels the endeavour is 'doomed to failure', because of the difficulty, perhaps even the impossibility, of communication between the sexes.

The unnamed man she addresses is middle-aged, prosperous and hard-working. He comes from the same social class as she does, so they would have no trouble in making polite conversation over dinner. But, Woolf says, there is one major difference between them which makes an unbridgeable gap' . . . you began your education at one of the great public schools and finished it at the university'.

She acknowledges that the sexes have many instincts in common, but:

> . . . to fight has always been the man's habit, not the woman's . . . Scarcely a human being in the course of history has fallen to a woman's rifle; the vast majority of birds and beasts have been killed by you, not us.

(Three Guineas, p.9)

History has shown that men's education has been singularly unsuccessful in promoting either a respect for liberty or a hatred of war, and this presents her with a difficulty. Women must have equal access to education, but what should this education consist of?

Pupils of the famous public school, Westminster. In Three Guineas, *Woolf returned to the theme of the inequalities between boys' and girls' education.*

A Cambridge proctor and his 'bulldogs'. Men's education was steeped in tradition.

Woolf has been asked to contribute to a fund for re-building a women's college which is in need of repair. She wants to stipulate that her donation be used to establish an experimental college for women, where only arts such as medicine, mathematics, music, painting and literature would be taught – in opposition to men's colleges which promote: 'the arts of ruling, killing, of acquiring land and capital'. She would like to scorn examinations and university degrees, but is aware that women graduating from such a college would be at a grave disadvantage when it came to applying for jobs. Without qualifications, women would not be able to earn their own livings, so marriage would remain their only option. Furthermore, if women remain dependent on the social system she is criticizing, they will have no power or influence to prevent wars.

The daughters of educated men escaped from their sheltered lives during the Great War by working in fields

Women escaped from the home to work in munitions factories like this one during the First World War, as Woolf pointed out.

and munitions factories, by driving lorries and nursing the wounded. But, according to Woolf, this was not real emancipation because it was dependent on a war begun and fought by men, and women must use their influence for peace.

Woolf's conclusion is that rebuilding the original college for women along the lines of men's colleges is the only option. She recognizes all the imperfections of this scheme, but donates her first guinea to the honorary treasurer of the building fund anyway: 'because by so doing we are making a positive contribution to the prevention of war'.

The 'three guineas' are symbolic, in the same way that the 'room of one's own and five hundred pounds a year' were in the earlier work. Her first guinea, then, goes to help educate the daughters of educated men, her second to help them earn their own livings in professions, and thus gain independence, and ultimately influence. The third guinea goes to the 'Society for Combating Fascism' – again, in a qualified way, for she refuses to join the Society herself. Her correspondent thinks war is evil, as she does herself: but he is a man, she is a woman, their ways of destroying evil must be different:

> We can best help you to prevent war by not joining your society but by remaining outside your society but in co-operation with its aim. That aim is the same for us both. It is to assert 'the rights of all – all men and women – to the respect in their persons of the great principles of Justice and Equality and Liberty'.

Opposite Women at Girton College, Cambridge. *In* Three Guineas, *Woolf decides that women can make the best progress by remaining outside male-orientated society. As she wrote in* A Room of One's Own: *'I thought how unpleasant it is to be locked out; and I thought how it is worse perhaps to be locked in.'*

(*Three Guineas*, p.164)

In *A Room of One's Own*, Woolf argued that the fact that women were locked out of the privileges of the men's colleges, could be turned to their advantage. In *Three Guineas* she makes a positive choice to remain outside a male-orientated society, since from this vantage-point, she believes, one can properly observe the problem of inequalities between men and women.

Virginia Woolf was one of the most important writers of the twentieth century. Her achievement lies in her willingness to take risks, to experiment with form and subject matter. In *Granite and Rainbow* she summed up her ideas of what a novelist should try to do, and in

doing so she described her own aims:

> . . . the most characteristic qualities of the novel – that it registers the slow growth and development of feeling, that it follows many lives and traces their unions and fortunes over a long stretch of time – are the very qualities that are most incompatible with design and order. It is the gift of style, arrangement, construction to put us at a distance from the special life and obliterate its features; while it is the gift of the novel to bring us into close touch with life . . . The most complete novelist must be the novelist who can balance the two powers so that the one enhances the other.

Stephen Tomlin's bust of Virginia Woolf, (1882-1941).

Glossary

Aesthetic Artistically pleasing; pleasing to the senses.

Androgeny Male and female characteristics balanced equally in one person.

Autobiography An account of a life written by the person who actually lived it.

Barbarian Someone who is uncivilized, savage and threatening.

Biography An account of a life written by someone other than the subject of it – for example, Quentin Bell wrote a biography of his aunt, Virginia Woolf.

Bloomsbury Group Bloomsbury is the part of London near the British Museum which includes Gordon Square, where Virginia and Vanessa lived after their father's death. The friends who met there became known as 'The Bloomsbury Group'. They had no real aims in common beyond a belief in the importance of the arts.

Delirium A disordered mental state, often as a result of fever or very high temperature.

Elusive Difficult to pin down or define.

Feudal system A social order prevalent in Western Europe between the ninth and sixteenth centuries which depended on class-consciousness: peasants who worked the land were dependent on the landowners for their homes and wages.

Freud, Sigmund (1856–1939). The Austrian founder of psychoanalysis. This is a method of enquiry into patients' minds to discover causes for nervous or hysterical illnesses. Freud discovered that patients who have had a disturbing experience may 'forget' it in their conscious waking lives; but it remains, repressed, in their unconscious. By discussing dreams and encouraging free association of words or ideas, Freud hoped to bring such repressed memories to light, effecting a cure.

Great War This is what the First World War (1914–18) was known as before the Second World War (1939–45) took place.

Interior monologue Writing which seems to record everything which is going on in a character's mind: some of which is important to the action of the novel; but also irrelevant thoughts which intrude. Writers like James Joyce, Marcel Proust and Woolf tried to capture the complexity of thought in this way.

Intuition The ability to understand, or see the truth of something, instinctively, without logical reasoning.

Jung, Carl (1875–1961). The Swiss pschoanalyst. Jung developed his theories along different lines from Freud. He believed that each individual shares in a 'collective unconscious' – a sort of inherited memory – as well as having private and personal memories.

Narrator The story-teller.

Narrative comment This is when the story-telling voice gives us information directly, rather than allowing it to emerge from the action of the story, or from characters' thoughts or conversation. In Woolf's fiction the narrative voice often follows a character's point of view so closely that it is difficult to tell whether an observation is a character's or a narrator's.

Objective time Measurements of time about which there is common scientific agreement, such as clock time, and calendar time.

Pageant A dramatic performance, usually taking place outside. Pageants differ from plays in that there is more emphasis on visual spectacle.

Parenthetic Additional information placed within a sentence in brackets.

Repression (see **Freud**) Banishing something that is too painful to think about to the unconscious part of the mind.

Sackville-West, Vita (1892–1962). English poet and novelist. Virginia Woolf met her in 1922 and they became intimate friends. Vita was the only child of Lionel, Lord Sackville, so the family seat, Knole, passed to a male cousin when he died in 1928, the year *Orlando* was published.

Stream of consciousness A term sometimes used instead of 'interior monologue' (see above).

Suffrage The right to vote. In the nineteenth century, women known as suffragists campaigned for votes for women, using only respectable methods. After 1903, 'suffragettes' (members of the Women's Social and Political Union) took up the campaign in a more militant way. Women over 30 were granted the vote in 1918, but equality with men was not won until 1928, when women over twenty-one could vote.

Unconscious   The deepest level of our minds, of which we are not aware.

List of dates

1878	Leslie Stephen and Julia Duckworth married.
1879	Vanessa Stephen was born.
1880	Thoby Stephen was born.
1882	Adeline Virginia Stephen born on 25 January. (James Joyce was born in Dublin on 2 February 1882.)
1895	Julia Stephen, Virginia's mother, died; Virginia suffered a nervous breakdown.
1897	Stella, Virginia's step-sister, married Jack Hills in April and died in July.
1902	Leslie Stephen was knighted.
1904	Leslie Stephen died in February; Virginia's second serious breakdown began in May. In December Virginia joined Vanessa in their new house, 46 Gordon Square in Bloomsbury, London.
1906	In September Vanessa and Virginia joined Adrian and Thoby in Greece; Thoby returned to London early because of illness and died of typhoid fever in November.
1907	Vanessa – who had been ill when Thoby was the year before – married Clive Bell in February. Virginia and Adrian moved to 29 Fitzroy Square.
1909	Lytton Strachey proposed to Virginia, but had second thoughts the following day.
1910	Virginia began doing voluntary work for Women's Suffrage. The first Post-Impressionist exhibition was organized by Roger Fry in London. This was an important event in the art world, and may have been one of the reasons Virginia wrote 'All human relations have shifted . . . Let us agree to place one of these changes about the year 1910.'
1912	Virginia married Leonard Woolf on 10 August.

1913	Suffering from depression and delusions, Virginia attempted suicide in September.
1914	The First World War started in August with the German invasion of Belgium. Joyce's *Dubliners* was published.
1915	The Woolfs moved into Hogarth House, Richmond. *The Voyage Out* was published in March by Duckworth (owned by Virginia's stepbrother Gerald). Virginia was very unwell in April and May.
1916	Joyce's *A Portrait of the Artist as a Young Man* was published.
1917	The Woolfs bought a printing press.
1918	Virginia met T.S. Eliot, who became a close friend. (End of the First World War.)
1919	The Woolfs bought Monk's House in Rodmell, Sussex. *Night and Day* was published by Duckworth.
1922	*Jacob's Room* was published by The Hogarth Press, so was T.S. Eliot's *The Waste Land*. (Joyce's *Ulysses* was published in Paris.)
1924	Vita Sackville-West took Virginia to visit Knole – (which eventually formed the background for *Orlando*). Virginia's essay 'Mr Bennett and Mrs Brown' was published. (E.M. Forster's *A Passage to India* was published.)
1925	*The Common Reader* and *Mrs Dalloway* were published.
1926	The Woolfs went to visit Thomas Hardy; in November they dined with H.G.Wells in order to meet Arnold Bennett.
1927	*To the Lighthouse* was published.
1928	*Orlando* was published. Virginia gave lectures in Cambridge on 'Women and Fiction'.
1929	Virginia's Cambridge lectures were published as *A Room of One's Own*.
1931	*The Waves* was published.
1932	*The Common Reader: Second Series* was published. Lytton Strachey died.
1933	*Flush* was published.
1937	*The Years* was published. Julian Bell, Virginia's nephew, died in the Spanish Civil War; he had volunteered to work as an ambulance driver.

1938	*Three Guineas* was published.
1939	The Woolfs visited Sigmund Freud – not for medical reasons. He gave Virginia a narcissus.
	England declared war on Germany on 3 September. James Joyce's *Finnegans Wake* was published.
1940	Virginia's biography of Roger Fry was published.
1941	Virginia finished writing *Between the Acts*, although it was not published until after her death. She drowned herself on 28 March after a month of severe depression. (James Joyce, who was born nine days after Virginia Woolf, died in the same year as she did, on 13 January 1941.)

Further reading

Works
Virginia Woolf's major works are all available in Granada paperbacks.
The Voyage Out, 1915
Night and Day, 1919
Jacob's Room, 1922
Mrs Dalloway, 1925
To the Lighthouse 1927
Orlando, 1928
A Room of One's Own, 1929
The Waves, 1931
Flush: A Biography, (of Elizabeth Barrett Browning's dog), 1933
The Years 1937
Three Guineas 1938
Roger Fry: A Biography, 1940
Between the Acts, 1941

Short stories
DICK, S. (ed:) *The Complete Short Stories of Virginia Woolf* (The Hogarth Press, 1985)
Woolf had published short stories in magazines and journals like *The Athenaeum, London Mercury, Criterion and Dial*. After her death some of these were published by The Hogarth Press under the title *A Haunted House and other Short Stories* in 1943.

Diaries and letters
In 1953 Leonard Woolf edited extracts from Virginia's diaries under the title *A Writer's Diary*. They have since been edited by Anne Olivier Bell in five volumes, and are available in Penguin paperbacks:

The Diary of Virginia Woolf, volume I: 1915-1919 (1979)
volume II: 1920-1924 (1981)
volume III: 1925-1930 (1982)
volume IV: 1931-1935 (1983)
volume V: 1936-1941 (1985)

Woolf's letters, edited by Nigel Nicholson, are published by the Hogarth Press in six volumes:
The Letters of Virginia Woolf: The Flight of the Mind volume I: 1888-1912
The Question of Things Happening, volume II: 1912-1922
A Change of Perspective, volume III: 1923-1928
A Reflection of the Other Person, volume IV
The Sickle Side of the Moon, volume V
Leave the Letters Till We're Dead, volume VI

See also SHULKIND, J. (ed.) *Moments of Being, Unpublished Autobiographical Writings of Virginia Woolf* (Triad Panther, 1978)

Woolf's essays and criticism
During her lifetime Woolf published two volumes of essays and criticism: *The Common Reader* in 1925 , and *The Common Reader: Second Series* in 1932. These included essays on Daniel Defoe, Jane Austen, the Brontë sisters, Joseph Conrad, James Joyce and Thomas Hardy. After her death these and other essays were published by The Hogarth Press under the following titles:
The Moment and Other Essays, 1947
The Captain's Death Bed and Other Essays, 1950
Granite and Rainbow, 1958
Contemporary Writers, 1965.
There are four volumes of *Collected Essays* which appeared from 1966–1967.

Biography and criticism
BELL, QUENTIN *Virginia Woolf, A Biography Volume One, Virginia Stephen, 1882–1912* (The Hogarth Press; Triad/

Granada, 1976)

BELL, QUENTIN *Virginia Woolf, A Biography Volume Two, Mrs Woolf, 1912–1941* (The Hogarth Press, 1972; Triad/ Granada, 1976)

MAJUMDAR, R. and McLAURIN, A. *The Critical Heritage,* (Routledge and Kegan Paul, 1975)

MARCUS, J. *New Feminist Essays on Virginia Woolf* (Macmillan, 1981)

POOLE, ROGER *The Unknown Virginia Woolf* (Cambridge University Press, 1978; Harvester Press, 1982)

ROSE, PHYLLIS *Woman of Letters* (Routledge and Kegan Paul, 1978)

ROSENBLATT, AARON *Virginia Woolf for Beginners* (Writers and Readers Publishing, 1987)

SPRAGUE, C. *Virginia Woolf, A Collection of Critical Essays* (Prentice Hall Inc., 1971)

Index

Picture acknowledgements

The author and publishers would like to thank the following for allowing their illustrations to be reproduced in this book: BBC Enterprises 59, 62, 64, 66, 67, 69, 70, 73; BBC Hulton Picture Library 44; The Billie Love Historical Collection 34, 36, 39, 43; The Mansell Collection 41; Mary Evans Picture Library 25, 28, 31, 32, 35, 50, 52–3, 56, 89, 90; The Mistress and Fellows, Girton College, Cambridge 86, 87, 97; The National Portrait Gallery 98; Popperfoto 22, 30, 37, 48, 74, 76, 95; Tate Gallery Archive, Vanessa Bell Collection 7, 8, 9, 10, 13, 14, 15, 16, 18, 19, 20, 21, 23, 26, 60, 61, 78–9, 84; Topham Picture Library 33, 47, 54, 81, 85, 93, 94; University of Sussex 83.